AMAZING ANIMALS

AXOLOTLS

BY ASHLEY GISH

CREATIVE EDUCATION • CREATIVE PAPERBACKS

Published by Creative Education
and Creative Paperbacks
P.O. Box 227, Mankato, Minnesota 56002
Creative Education and Creative Paperbacks
are imprints of The Creative Company
www.thecreativecompany.us

Design by The Design Lab
Production by Blue Design
Art direction by Graham Morgan

Images by Getty Images/Kaan Sezer, 21, Kevin Schafer, 9, Paul Starosta, 5, 6; Pexels/Artem Lysenko, 2; Shutterstock/Eric Isselee, cover, 1; Unsplash/Chantal Bodmer, 10, Nathan, 17; Wikimedia Commons/Amandasofiarana, 20, Bouboulski, 23, Brandon Antonio Segura Torres & Priscilla Vieto Bonilla, 14, DataBase Center for Life Science (DBCLS), 8, Nico-c1amour, 18, LoKiLeCh, 13, Loukus999, 7, Orizatriz, 16

Cataloging-in-Publication data is available from the Library of Congress.
Library Binding ISBN: 9798895810521
Paperback ISBN: 9798896800057
eBook ISBN: 9798895811788
LCCN: 2025011186

Printed in the United States of America

Table of Contents

Axolotls can change their color to hide from predators.

The mysterious axolotl (ACK-suh-LAH-tuhl) looks like an alien. But it is a kind of **amphibian**. It lives its whole life underwater. In 2025, there were fewer than 1,000 axolotls living in the wild. But they are popular pets.

amphibian cold-blooded animal whose babies live in water

The word "axolotl" means "water dog." Axolotls are named for the Aztec god Xolotl.

Feathery **gills** stick out like ears on the sides of the axolotl's head. Its tail is shaped like a paddle. Wild axolotls are gray or brown. Pet axolotls may be pink, yellow, or black.

gill an organ that pulls oxygen from water

Adult axolotls are about 6 to 18 inches (15–46 centimeters) long. They have a good sense of smell. But they have poor eyesight. Besides breathing through their gills, axolotls can also breathe through their lungs, and even their skin!

Axolotls do not have teeth.

Wild axolotls can be found only in Lake Xochimilco in Mexico. They stay safe during the day by burrowing under the mud at the bottom of the lake. They come out to hunt for food at night.

As of 2025, there were between 50 and 1,000 axolotls in the wild.

Axolotls have small ridges on their head and cheeks. The ridges sense movement in the water. This helps axolotls find food. They eat worms, snails, insects, and small fish.

Axolotls are not friendly with each other. Young axolotls may even try to eat each other!

In the wild, snakes, birds, and fish eat baby axolotls.

Axolotl mothers lay hundreds of eggs. The eggs hatch in two weeks. Baby axolotls are called **larvae** (LAR-vay). After about nine days, the larvae grow front legs. A few weeks later, they grow back legs.

larvae baby axolotls

After growing back legs, young axolotls look like small copies of their parents. The young axolotls can lay eggs of their own by six months of age. Axolotls can live for up to 25 years.

Axolotls keep growing bigger during their whole lifetime.

Other amphibians that keep some baby features are the siren, olm, and Lake Patzcuaro salamander.

Axolotls are one of just a few amphibians that do not complete **metamorphosis** (MEH-tuh-MOR-fuh-sis). This is why adults do not lose their baby gills, webbed feet, and flat tail as they grow up.

metamorphosis growing new body parts while changing from baby to adult

Axolotls have the amazing ability to regrow just about any body part, including their legs, tail, heart, and lungs. Scientists want to figure out how to use this ability to grow human organs for sick people who need them.

Farming and water pollution are some reasons why so few axolotls survive in the wild.

An Axolotl Tale

The Aztec gods chose one god, Xolotl, to protect the sun at night. But he ran away. He hid himself by changing into an axolotl. When the other gods found him, they made him protect the sun every night, forever.

Read More

Bowman, Chris. *The Ultimate Animal Library: Axolotls*. Minnetonka, MN: Blastoff! Readers, 2025.

Daniels, Ruby. *Odd But Adorable Animals: Axolotls*. North Mankato, MN: 2024

Doty, Abby. *Creepy Creatures: Axolotls*. Mendota Heights, MN: Northstar Editions, 2025.

Websites

Axolotl
https://animals.sandiegozoo.org/animals/axolotl
Read more about axolotls on the San Diego Zoo website.

Mexican Axolotl
https://kids.nationalgeographic.com/animals/amphibians/facts/mexican-axolotl
Learn more about Mexican axolotls on National Geographic Kids.

Note: Every effort has been made to ensure that the websites listed above are suitable for children, that they have educational value, and that they contain no inappropriate material. However, because of the nature of the Internet, it is impossible to guarantee that these sites will remain active indefinitely or that their contents will not be altered.

Index